Make It a Party

with Sizzix®

TECHNIQUES AND IDEAS FOR USING DIE-CUTTING AND EMBOSSING MACHINES

Creative Publishing
international

Quarto is the authority on a wide range of topics.
Quarto educates, entertains and enriches the lives of our readers—enthusiasts and lovers of hands-on living.
www.QuartoKnows.com

ELLISON EDUCATIONAL EQUIPMENT, INC.
25862 COMMERCENTRE DRIVE
LAKE FOREST, CALIFORNIA 92630
www.sizzix.com
Ellison® & Sizzix® are trademarks of Ellison Educational Equipment, Inc.
©2015 Ellison

Customer Service Hours
6:30 a.m. to 4:00 p.m., Pacific Time, Monday through Friday

By Phone
877-355-4766
(Toll Free in the USA)
949-598-8821
(Outside of the USA)

215 Historic 25th Street, Ogden, Utah 84401

First published in the United States of America in 2016 by
Creative Publishing international, a member of
Quarto Publishing Group USA Inc.
100 Cummings Center
Suite 406-L
Beverly, Massachusetts 01915-6101
Telephone: 978-282-9590
Fax: 978-283-2742
QuartoKnows.com
Visit our blogs at QuartoKnows.com

10 9 8 7 6 5 4 3 2 1
ISBN: 978-1-58923-933-3

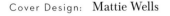

Cover Design: **Mattie Wells**

Design Production: **Lisa Ballard**

Photographer: **Ryne Hazen, Hazen Photography**

Copy Editor: **Cynthia Levens**

Kristin Highberg

FOREWORD

When I think of parties, I tend to think of the people who make them so special.

But looking back, it's obvious that the atmosphere really sets the mood for celebrating all the things that matter most to us.

In *Make It a Party* with Sizzix, you're invited to our biggest, most-inspiring bash yet. Discover our very best tips and techniques for using our award-winning die-cutting and embossing machines to design the perfect cards, decorations, favors, and gift packaging.

These amazing ideas come directly from our in-house and online design teams, licensed designers, and a few of our closest friends who have done all the planning for you—down to the last fun detail.

So what are you waiting for? Let's get this party started right now!

Happy Crafting,

Kristin Highberg
Chief Executive Officer
Ellison/Sizzix

CHAPTER **3**

Party Décor

CHAPTER **4**

Party Accessories

How-To

Welcome to the World of Sizzix®

As one of the DIY market's most requested brands, we continue to develop award-winning products with unsurpassed quality to empower expression in all. We invite each and every individual to explore their artistic potential through our family of die-cutting and embossing machines that produce many beautiful designs to suit any style.

From scrapbooking, cardmaking, and papercrafting to fashion, quilting, and home décor, we provide makers of all ages and abilities the opportunity to express themselves in countless new creative ways.

Ideas from the Experts

Beginning Crafters Welcome!

Each project in this book can be uniquely made and remade with ease, no matter your level of experience. Whether you replicate a project exactly or are inspired by certain elements or it takes your imagination away to new areas of creativity, you're sure to enjoy what follows.

Partygoers will be amazed at the ingenuity and innovation that these creations convey in a variety of celebratory themes. You'll be constantly challenged to take your creativity further with projects that make any event truly eventful.

Celebrating Creativity

Rather than taking you through each project step-by-step, this idea book was meant to inspire your own party planning vision. For added ease, many project photos are accompanied by helpful hints, including a list of the Sizzix items used and special notes detailing tips and techniques to showcase your style.

Inspiring Essentials

Sizzix tools offer the advantages of award-winning art plus perfectly cut or embossed shapes every time! Imagine the advantages of cutting out embellishments for dozens of party invitations in mere minutes. Or how about making elegant professional-quality embossed impressions in an instant? With Sizzix, it's just that easy!

Our chemically-etched dies cut a single sheet of thin material such as cardstock—the more intricate the design, the more amazing the die-cut! Our steel-rule dies offer even more versatility, cutting materials like fabric, burlap, foam, felt, mat board, craft metal, and more for the most personalized projects to complement your creativity.

Getting Started

**Making a Basic Sizzix®
Sandwich Using Wafer-Thin,
Chemically-Etched Dies**

Place material to be die-cut on Cutting Pad. Place die over material and align. Place another Cutting Pad over the die and material to create a "sandwich." Place sandwich on Extended Multipurpose Platform and slide the Platform into the opening of the machine. Note the rotation of the handle and continue to rotate it in the same direction until the sandwich has passed through the opening of the rollers. Remove the sandwich from the machine. Your die-cut shape is ready to use!

Using Framelits,™ Thinlits™ or other Wafer-Thin Dies

Die

Cutting Pads

Single Sheet of Paper or Cardstock

Extended Multipurpose Platform (Tab 2)

MACHINES

Big Shot™ | BIGkick™

With a 6"-wide opening, this versatile die-cutting machine really is the hub of any crafter's universe. As a portable roller machine, it easily cuts and embosses many different materials. Create your own one-of-a-kind cards, invitations, scrapbook pages, home décor, fashion, altered art, quilting, and much more!

Big Shot™ Plus

It's everything you love about the Big Shot – plus even more value. With a brand new 9" size opening for expanded creativity, this versatile machine easily accommodates all 8 1/2" x 11" materials for even bigger possibilities!

Big Shot™ Pro

For the crafter who wants it all, comes the pro-strength machine that does it all. From our embossing folders to our smallest dies to our biggest 12" Bigz™ Pro dies, the Big Shot Pro machine works with any Sizzix® die or embossing folder to create an amazing assortment of craft shapes.

Vagabond™

Inspired by Tim Holtz®, the Vagabond machine easily opens up to reveal a portable yet powerful machine that takes you to imaginative new places. Upon closer examination, the Vagabond impresses with its uncanny ability to effortlessly cut and emboss many different materials and thicknesses.

Texture Boutique™

Make an unforgettable impression! This amazing cardmaking and embellishing system elegantly transforms ordinary cardstock into one-of-a-kind embossed art that showcases our deepest and richest textures.

TECHNOLOGY

steel-rule

Look out for Bigz™, Originals™, On the Edge™, and Movers & Shapers™ dies. These will cut a wide range of materials, making them perfect for papercrafting, home décor, quilting, and more!

Cuts:
- cardstock
- felt
- fabric
- foam
- magnet
- leather
- craft aluminum
- chipboard
- metallic foil
- and much more!

wafer-thin

Our Framelits™ and Thinlits™ dies are perfect for layering and cutting apertures and a whole host of intricate shapes that will make your papercrafting really stand out from the crowd!

Cuts:
- cardstock
- paper
- metallic foil
- vellum

chemically-etched

Check out our Sizzlits® and Embosslits™. Designed to cut a single sheet of cardstock, Sizzlits create fabulous little shapes that make a great big difference with your papercrafting. Go one step further with Embosslits – these clever little dies cut AND emboss for some very impressive results!

Cuts:
- cardstock
- paper
- metallic foil
- vellum

embossing folders

Our Textured Impressions™ Embossing Folders have male (raised) and female (recessed) surfaces on opposite sides of a folder. When it is passed through a die-cutting or embossing machine, the folder applies pressure to cardstock to alter the surface, giving it a raised effect.

Molded plastic embossing folders do not cut paper. These folders only emboss and are designed to be used with a single sheet of thin material.

quilting/ appliqué

This exclusive collection of dies allows you to create personalized quilts and patchwork masterpieces, taking away the sometimes laborious task of using a ruler and rotary cutter. The collection features some of the most popular quilt shapes, including standard squares and triangles, as well as Apple Core, Dresden Plate, Drunkard's Path, and much more!

You can cut multiple layers of fabric at any one time with these hardy and versatile dies, giving you a precise and clean cut every time. They even come with a built-in 1/4" seam allowance to make piecing by hand or machine even easier!

Textured Impressions

Textured Impressions Embossing Folders offer the deepest and boldest embossing experience. You can turn ordinary cardstock, paper, metallic foil, or vellum into an embossed, textured masterpiece. The large folder also fits the exact dimensions of an A2 or A6 card, while the small, medium, or border sizes create amazing embellishments.

Accessories

Our complete line of accessories will further enhance your creative life. Make creating easier with our Magnetic Platform, Stamper's Secret Weapon™, and Tool Kit. Embrace efficiency by using our Cut & Emboss Paper and Mat Board Packs. Expand your creative potential with Embossing Diffusers™ and the Dimensional Cutting Pad. And don't forget to keep your crafting tools organized with our Die & Embossing Storage!

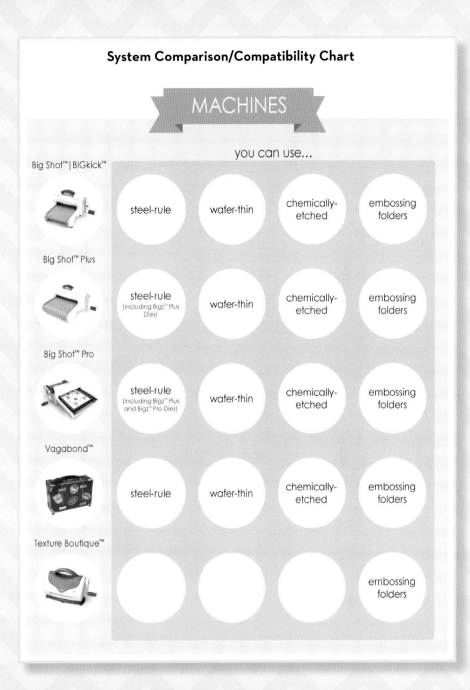

System Comparison/Compatibility Chart

MACHINES

you can use...

	steel-rule	wafer-thin	chemically-etched	embossing folders
Big Shot™ | BIGkick™	steel-rule	wafer-thin	chemically-etched	embossing folders
Big Shot™ Plus	steel-rule (including Bigz™ Plus Dies)	wafer-thin	chemically-etched	embossing folders
Big Shot™ Pro	steel-rule (including Bigz™ Plus and Bigz™ Pro Dies)	wafer-thin	chemically-etched	embossing folders
Vagabond™	steel-rule	wafer-thin	chemically-etched	embossing folders
Texture Boutique™				embossing folders

Tips & Tricks

Page 39
Project #5 – When die-cutting vellum, make sure to use an adhesive that is clear or an adhesive designed to use with vellum so it doesn't distract from your project.

Page 46
Project #3 – Apply adhesive to decorative shapes in an adhesive machine like Xyron. When you remove the protective backing of the adhesive, glitter will stick very easily.

Page 32
Project #1 – Always use fabric or paper printed on two sides when creating a project where the back or the inside will be seen as much as the front or the outside.

Page 40
Project #6 – Cover your mat board in patterned paper before die-cutting. It will save a step and eliminate the need to line up designs later.

Page 49
Project #7 – When mass-producing a particular box for a party, create an assembly line so you do all the cutting first, then assembly, and finally embellishing. It will make the process go faster.

Page 52

Project #1 – When creating rosettes, it is best to use a strong adhesive like hot glue to securely close the rosette.

Page 60

Project #3 – An easy way to transfer your vinyl cutouts is to use a vinyl transfer tape. It will help with placement and making things straight.

Page 57

Project #4 – When making food picks or photo props on sticks, make sure to cut matching die-cuts so both sides of the stick are decorated.

Page 60

Project #1 – When creating dimensional flowers, alternative materials such as wrapping paper or tissue paper offer great texture and pattern.

Page 67

Project #4 – Use the negative space of a shape on a project to add visual interest and dimension.

Page 73
Project #6 – Use a sewing machine and a straight stitch to make a fast and easy garland. Idea: Cover stitching with bead stickers.

Page 83
Project #4 – Long border dies or decorative strips can be used to make a variety of paper chains.

Page 78
Project #1 – Use a store-bought item as the base of your project. Use decorative die-cuts to personalize it with the colors and papers you want.

Page 80
Project #3 – Create a stencil from a decorative shape that creates a good silhouette. Apply removable adhesive to the stencil. Place the stencil on the material you want and use acrylic paint to fill in the stencil.

Page 85
Project #5 – If you don't have the best hand printing, use a computer-generated font to trace and transfer onto a chalkboard for a title.

Page 90
Project #1 – Use the top-fold technique to create a stand-up card out of a 2-D shape. Use a piece of paper twice as long as the die design to be cut. Fold the paper in half. Lay the folded edge of the paper just inside the cutting rule of the top of the design. Be sure the cutting rule extends above the edge of the fold.

Page 96
Project #1 – Decorative pinwheels are great for a centerpiece. You can create a working pinwheel by using a thumbtack in place of a brad. Insert the end of the thumbtack into the eraser of a pencil.

Page 112
Project #3 – Decorative metal foils are a fun material to die-cut. They can easily be molded and shaped. You can also use alcohol inks to add color and dimension.

Page 101
Project #7 – There are many great ways to highlight an embossed image. You can sand the raised embossed image to expose the colored or white core of the paper, or you can add dimension by adding chalk or rubber stamp ink.

CHAPTER 1

It's a Party!

Party ideas to create
the perfect party
complete with
everything from
invitations to table
decorations and
thank you notes,
and more ...

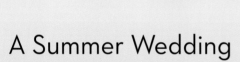

CONGRATULATIONS

A Summer Wedding

by Eileen Hull

SIZZIX DIES USED:

1 659871

2 657380

3 659871

4 659118

5

6

7

A Summer Wedding (CONT.)

by Eileen Hull

SIZZIX DIES USED:

5 658054

6 657114, 658053, 657119

7 657720

8 657726

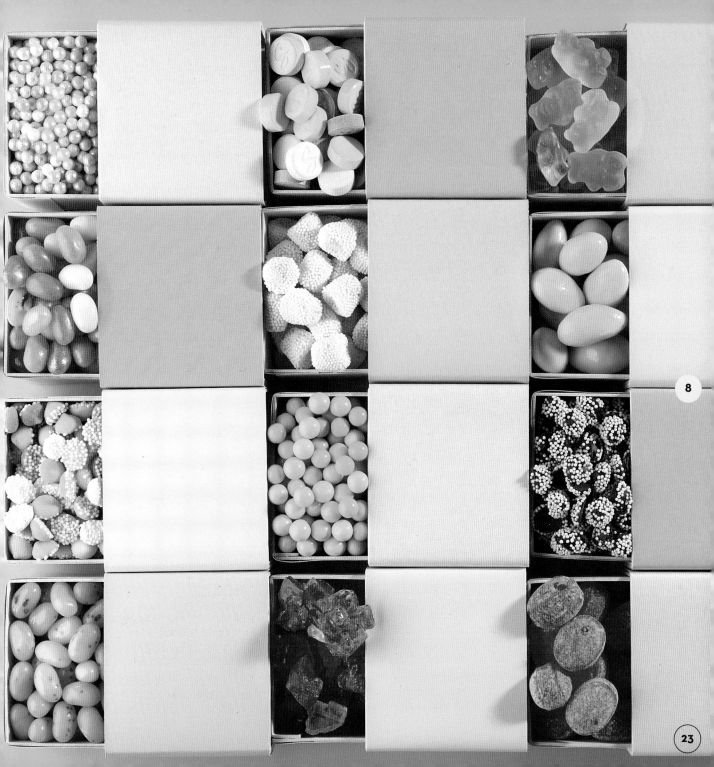

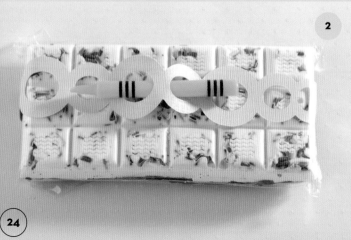

A Baby Shower

by Sizzix In-House Designers

SIZZIX DIES USED:

1 660292, 660261

2 659871

3 660261, 656931

A Baby Shower

(CONT.)

by Sizzix In-House Designers

SIZZIX DIES USED:

4 660289

5 660261

6 658986

7 660261, 658690

8 658690, 660289

Card Front

5 Card Back

4

6

Card Closed

thank you

7

8

photos

Card Open

A Birthday Party for Girls

by WHERE WOMEN COOK

SIZZIX DIES USED:

1 658101, 659539, 659541, 659937, 656784, 659184, 658771, 659740

2 659937

3 660891, 659871, 658771, 660895

SIZZIX DIES USED:

4 660893

5 660896

6 660891

7 658771, 660893, 659541, 659179, 660895

Celebrate a Very Merry Christmas

by Stephanie Ackerman

SIZZIX DIES USED:

1 660684

2 660682

3 660280

4 660679, 660677, 660895

It's the most
wonderful time of the year
for a Cookie Exchange

If you would like to exchange cookies,
please bring 2 dozen of your most
favorite Christmas Cookie
and a copy of your recipe.

Friday, December 11, 2015
at 7:00 pm
Stephanie's House

5

Celebrate a Very Merry Christmas (CONT.)

by Stephanie Ackerman

SIZZIX DIES USED:

5 660681, 660680, 660679

6 660678, 660273

7 660681, 660684

8 660679, 660684

9 660679

10 660280, 660678

11 660659

6

7

8

Chocolate Chip Cookies

1 cup butter
1 cup sugar
2 cups unpacked Brown Sugar
4 large eggs
2 tablespoons vanilla extract
2 teaspoons salt
2 teaspoons baking soda
5 1/2 cups flour
LOTS of Chocolate Chips (maybe 2 cups)

10

9

11

CHAPTER 2

Party
Paper
Goods

Party Paper Goods
include: Invitations,
Save-the-Date Cards,
Table Assignment
Cards, Tags,
Thank You Notes,
and more...

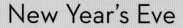

New Year's Eve

SIZZIX DIES USED:

1 657663, 657190

2 657190, 658332

3 660103

4 658983, 656931

5 660699, 659428

6 659942, 658279

SAVE *The* DATE

for a fabulous new year

12.31.2015

8 pm at The Mariano Home • 24631 Ballen Cove
Please bring a drink for cheering
& an appetizer for sharing
rsvp to Cara by 12/28 at 949-111-1234

4

5

6

GOOD LUCK

Valentine's Day

SIZZIX DIES USED:

1 657212

2 660796

3 658745

4 659858, 660233, 659859, 660209

5 656761, 657021

6 656492, 658054

7 659874, 656931

8 A11007

9 660787, 660790

10 659540

7

9

8

10

TABLE
3
WILSONS

Wedding Day

1

2

3

4

5

7

6

8

St. Patrick's Day/ Good Luck

SIZZIX DIES USED:

1 660164 - eshape®

2 eclips® Cartridge

3 658972, 658973

4 660330

5 659536, 659183, 659182, A11014

WE ARE LUCKY

To have such great friends and family!
Please join the O'Brien Family
for a
ST. PATRICK'S DAY PARTY!

March 17, 2016
6:00 pm
7 Shamrock Circle, Cork Republic of Ireland

RSVP Wendy @ 555-7777

GOOD LUCK ON YOUR TRIP!

Eileen Hull

with ♥

703. 283. 2012
1127 Devon Street
Herndon, VA 20170

Spring/Easter

SIZZIX DIES USED:

1 656492, 657720, 657000

2 658358

3 659249

4 660264

5 660310

6 658452

7 659189, 659426

4

5

6

7

1

2

3

Baby Shower

SIZZIX DIES USED:

1 660252

2 660256, 658332

3 655710, tiny heart stickers

4 658976

5 660895

6 660261

7 656491, 658987

HOORAY!

Jessica &
Jason Veara

ARE OVERJOYED TO ANNOUNCE THE BIRTH OF

WELCOME

Daniel Benjamin

* 2 JULY 2012 *
weighing 7 lbs. 3 oz.
and measuring
19 3/4 inches
10:52 am

④

⑤

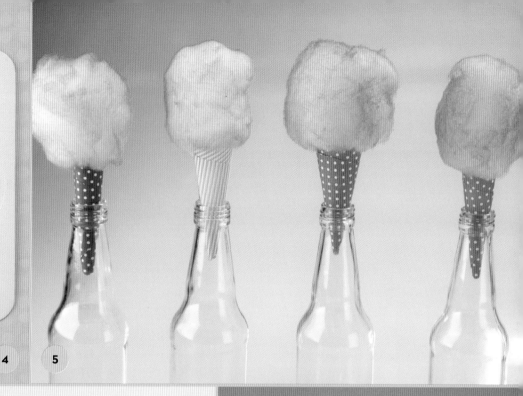

⑥

⑦

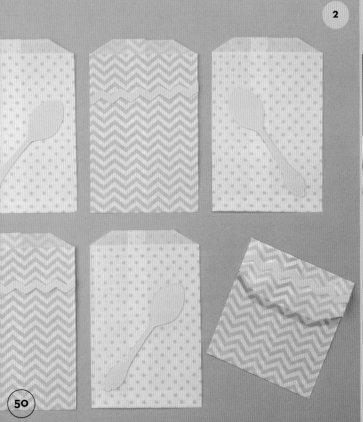

1st Birthday

SIZZIX DIES USED:

1 660261, 660252

2 657721, 659869, purchased bags

3 660783

4 659949, 660675

5 660290, 660296

6 658976

4

5

6

It's a Party!
October 25
5:30 p.m.
Mark's House

Happy Mother's Day

SIZZIX DIES USED:

1 659728

2 658053, 658563, 659645, 657712, 11073

3 659870, 658978

4 659188, 659650

5 658772, 658466, 656545

6 659538

Anniversaries

SIZZIX DIES USED:

1 659624

2 656938, 660211

3 659184, 656927

4 659532

5 659936

6 657951

7 959944, pop top for buckle

Please Join Us For Dinner

Friday, January 17, 2013
6 o'clock in the evening

at the Nelson home
4839 Sommerset Lane
Bishop, AZ

Hosted by Chris and Andrea Nelson

5

6

7

25th
WEDDING
ANNIVERSARY

May 19, 2015
7:00 p.m.

Please join Michael and Wendy in
the celebration of 25 years of
marriage.

HOTEL CALIFORNIA
LAGUNA BEACH, CA

1

2

To: Dad
Love you double
Olivia

To: Dad
Love you more
Jackson

3

eat

eat

eat

Happy Father's Day

SIZZIX DIES USED:

1 660330

2 657247

3 659198, 659192

4 659741, 659426, 659063

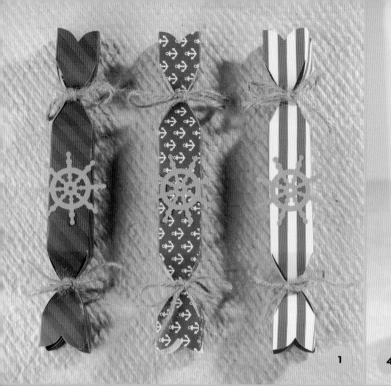

1

4

2

3

Remember the Butter

CHECK IT OUT →

MESSAGE IN A BOTTLE

Summer/Beach/ 4th of July

SIZZIX DIES USED:

1 658745, 660000

2 660007

3 660280, 660301

4 A10966

5 659187

6 660352

7 659180, 659531

5

6

7

Back-to-School for Tweens

SIZZIX DIES USED:

1 659242

2 656938, 659630, 660251, 657551

3 658563

4 659403, 659508, 655838, 658716, 660056

5 A11039

6 658784, 658988, 659090, 660239

7 A11023, A10598

8 659944, 658566

Card Front

Card Back

Keep On!

5

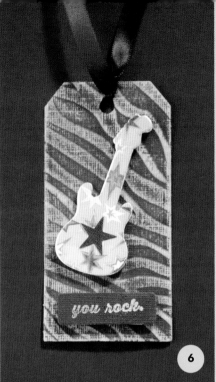

you rock.

6

7

8

2014 journal

you're invited

EPIC

AND IN THAT MOMENT, I SWEAR, WE WERE INFINITE

PLEASE JOIN US FOR A
PIZZA PARTY
celebrating the 10th
birthday of
DEVIN

Saturday, March 10
6 to 9 pm
ROBERTO'S PIZZERIA

WE ARE

Boys Birthday Party

SIZZIX DIES USED:

1 659870, 660331, 657182

2 657724, 656636

3 659783

4 660142

Girls Birthday Party

SIZZIX DIES USED:

1 660775, 660774

2 658502

3 658053

4 660420, 660414

5 659186, pre-made card

6 660233, 657884, 659934

7 660294

You're Invited

Date:
Time:
Place:

Card
Open

PARTY

Card
Closed

YOU ARE PEAR-FECT

4

6

5

7

A Maker Party

SIZZIX DIES USED:

1 660684

2 657671, 659769

3 659876, 658461

4 660411

5 660263, 660256, 658572,
   657212, 658568

6 660262, 660256

7 659711

4

5

6

i am simply me.
i am enough

7

Shine On

Bright Ideas

Fall/Halloween/
Thanksgiving

SIZZIX DIES USED:

1 656927, 657843

2 660011

3 660271, 660684

4 660994

5 659197, 658784

6 659186

7 657457, 660021

4

5

6

hard
pear
cider
&
cinnamon
doughnuts

hard
apple
cider
&
pumpkin
doughnuts

thanksgiving

7

CHAPTER 3

Party Décor

Party Décor Ideas include: Table Decorations and Settings, Hanging and Wall Décor, Decorative Wrapping Ideas for Gift Giving To Friends, Cake Toppers, and more ...

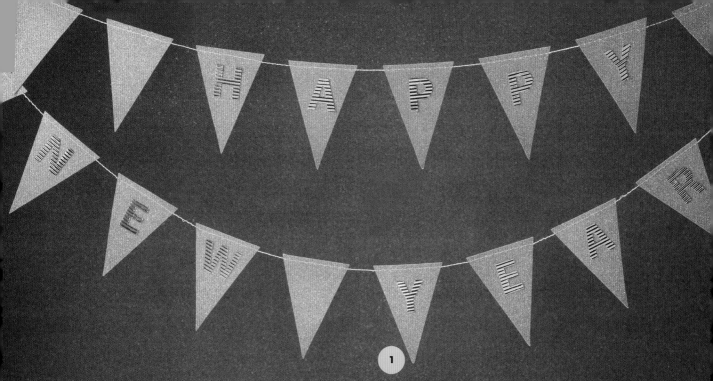

New Year's Eve

SIZZIX DIES USED:

1 658881

2 658053

3 657551

4 658881

5 660896

6 657551

3

4

5

6

Valentine's Day

SIZZIX DIES USED:

1 658917, computer-generated letters cut into squares

2 659624, 658339

3 656771, 660292, 659958

4 659916

5 A11007

6 A11007

Wedding Day

SIZZIX DIES USED:

1 A10120

2 657376, 657338, 657374

3 659195, 657021

4 657121

5 A10120

6 659184

1

2

3

4

5

6

St. Patrick's Day/ Good Luck

SIZZIX DIES USED:

1 659503, A10600

2 659191, 659182

3 658976

4 659708, 660021

4

Spring/Easter

SIZZIX DIES USED:

1 A11108

2 659874, 659871

3 657485

4 657485, 660056, 660256, 659653

Baby Shower

SIZZIX DIES USED:

1 657376   **4** 657565, 658563

2 660285   **5** 660892

3 660354   **6** 659871

4

5

6

1st Birthday

SIZZIX DIES USED:

1 659196

2 657551, small heart punch

3 658541, 657522, 10315

4 A10637

5 659605, 6592000

6 655128, 660056, 659928

Sea the Rainbow

4

aubrey turns 1

5

6

ONE WONDERFUL

1

2   **3**

Happy Mother's Day

SIZZIX DIES USED:

1 659620

2 655128

3 660893

4 659426, 658984

5 659621

6 659246

4

5

6

Anniversaries

SIZZIX DIES USED:

1 660195, 658554, 659940

2 660578

3 659197

4 659118

5 660260

6 660778

88

Happy Father's Day

SIZZIX DIES USED:

1 660262, 660223, 660210

2 659190

3 659939

4 660280

5 659185

6 656493, 660262, 660251, 659875

7 659537

Card Closed

Card Open

love

WE LOVE YOU PAPA BEAR!

4

5

6

7

BEST DAD AWARD

Summary / Beach / 4th of July

SIZZIX DIES USED:

1 660352, 660350

2 660352, 660350

3 659576, 660007

4 660138, A10966

4

Back-to-School for Tweens

SIZZIX DIES USED:

1 659892

2 659892, 659891

3 659198

4 659944

5 657721

6 659865, 659874, 659866

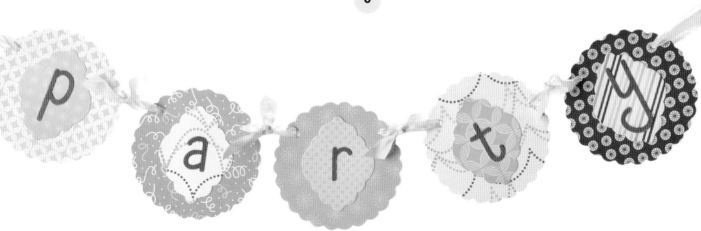

Boys Birthday Party

SIZZIX DIES USED:

1 660455

2 659944

3 656827

4 658058, 658553, 658772

5 660798

Girls Birthday Party

SIZZIX DIES USED:

1 658730, 660251

2 659543, 659542

3 659721, 660225, 659596

4 660260

5 659622

6 658051, A11014

7 660895

4

6

5

7

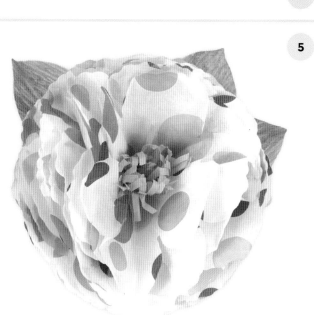

A Maker Party

SIZZIX DIES USED:

1 660895

2 659195

3 659181

4 660017

5 659181

6 660015

7 659185, 659194, 659199

8 659539

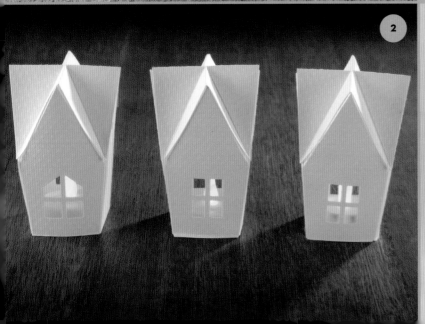

4

5

6

7

8

bubble yum

peach

cherry

Fall / Halloween / Thanksgiving

SIZZIX DIES USED:

1 658777, 658714, 658712   **4** 658745

2 658346   **5** 657725

3 659877, 657824

APPLE

CHERRY

PUMPKIN

PEACH

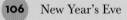
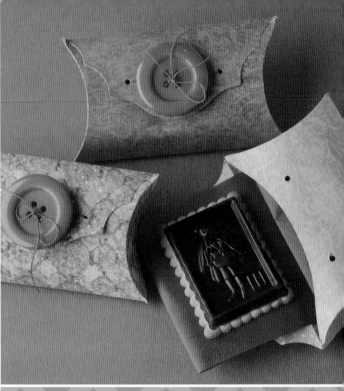

CHAPTER 4

Party Accessories

Party Accessory Ideas include: Table Settings – Straw, Bottle, and Cupcake Toppers – Coasters, Banners, Journals, Candy Boxes, Gift Wrapping, and more ....

1

2

New Year's Eve

SIZZIX DIES USED:

1 658745, 658761, 658034

2 656737, 659448

3 658761, 659508

4 660893

5 658533

6 659185, 659199, 659184

7 656546

MAY YOUR *New Year* SPARKLE

4

5

PROGRAM

6

7

congrats

Valentine's Day

SIZZIX DIES USED:

1 658050

2 656492, 658053, 658057, 658050

3 660452

4 659916, 660146

5 657719, 657375

6 657691, 659962, 660273, 657570, 657571, 655128, 659737

You make me happy

4

5

6

WISH

SIZZIX DIES USED:

1 660789, 660791, 660790

2 659624

3 656761, 657983, purchased boxes

4 A10154

5 660358, 660259, 659726

6 659188

7 659187, 659185, 659199

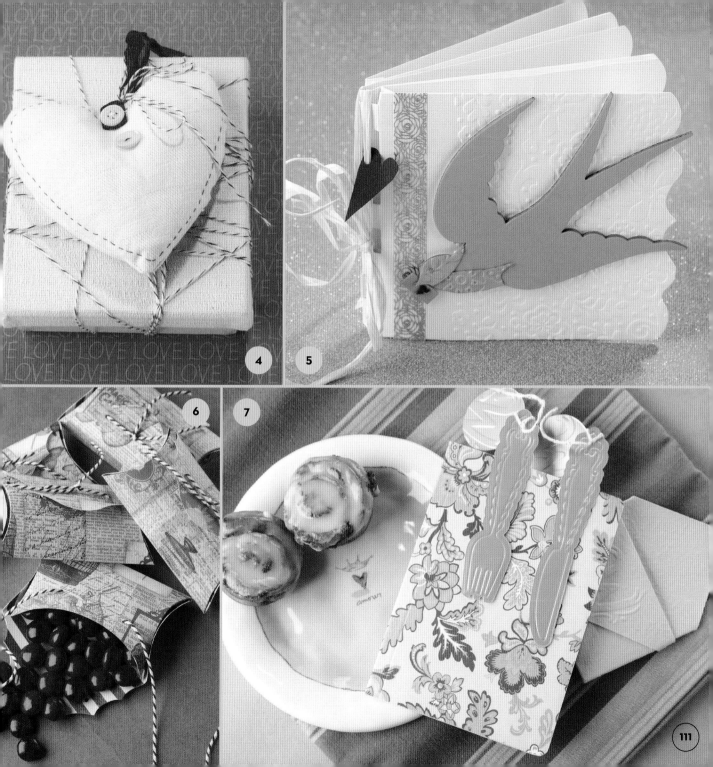

St. Patrick's Day/Good Luck

SIZZIX DIES USED:

1 659182, 659185

2 659198, 657841

3 657121, soda can

4 660104

5 659941

6 656212, wire to form word

7 659943

8 659789

5

7

6

8

Spring/Easter

SIZZIX DIES USED:

1 659540, 659242

2 660277

3 660265, 660264

Card Unfolded

Card Folded

Baby Shower

SIZZIX DIES USED:

1 658988, 657551, 657330, 658973

2 659871 (garland), 658984, 659866

3 656594, cut pie triangle from circle

4 655834

5 659540

6 660289, 657552

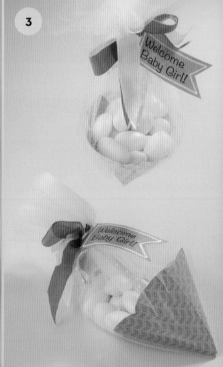

1

2

1st Birthday

SIZZIX DIES USED:

1 659927, 659930

2 660354, A11110

3 657012

3

Happy Mother's Day

SIZZIX DIES USED:

1 658356, 658339, 658340

2 659183

3 658966, 659531

4 659183

5 656544

6 657012, 656492, 658984, 657916

7 657121

8 657121

I WISH I MAY I WISH I MIGHT...

Anniversaries

SIZZIX DIES USED:

1 656339

2 659874, 657212

3 656492, 658056, 658052

4 657007, 657745, 657210

5 659188

6 657007, 656491, 658058, 658052

7 659198

8 659197, 660249, 657212, 660060

happiness

Happy Father's Day

SIZZIX DIES USED:

1 657724, 656142

2 658984

3 660295

4 659198, 659192

5 658562, 660265, 660264

6 659865, 657726, 659866

7 660295

8 657471, 659865, 657726

HAPPY FATHERS DAY
BBQ MASTER
HAPPY FATHERS DAY

4

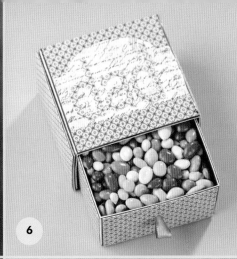

6

8

5

7

Summer / Beach / 4th of July

SIZZIX DIES USED:

1 659879, 659877, 658716, 657115, 659865

2 659180

3 660007, 659576

4 658739, 658332

5 656339

6 660360

Back-to-School for Tweens

SIZZIX DIES USED:

1 659891

2 660291, 659712

3 659185, 659194

4 659940

5 657842, 659925

6 659944

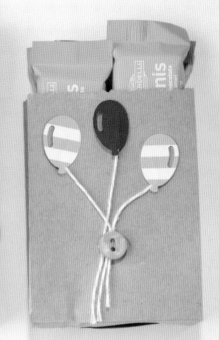

5

6

Boys Birthday Party

SIZZIX DIES USED:

1 657458

2 655710, 659753, 656802

3 659630, 659942

4 659874, 656491

5 656235

6 659188

7 A10647

3

1

2

4

6

5

it's your
SPECIAL DAY
lets Celebrate!

7

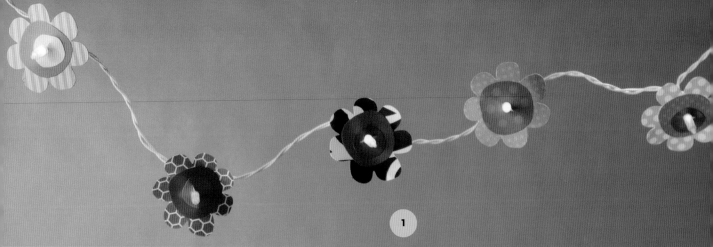

1

2

Girls
Birthday Party

SIZZIX DIES USED:

1 660277

2 A11024, A11003

3 A10647, 660260

4 659688, 660111

5 659531, 659196, 659243

6 660293

A Maker Party

SIZZIX DIES USED:

1 657209, 657007

2 657597, 659740, 659735

3 660310, 660301

4 A11002

5 660240

6 659769, 657671

7 659157 (cut square in half), brad

5

6

7

Fall / Halloween / Thanksgiving

SIZZIX DIES USED:

1 659621

2 657460, 658268

3 660784, 660781, 659895, 659949

4 660700, 660652

CONTRIBUTORS

Brenda Walton
I am a graphic designer, illustrator, and calligrapher. After graduating with a master's degree in studio art from California State University, Sacramento, I continued my studies in painting and calligraphy in London, New York, and San Francisco. While raising my newborn son, my husband and I launched a design business specializing in custom hand-lettered wedding invitations and logo types. I now partner with leading manufacturers to create products for social expression, crafting, and entertaining. Visit my blog: www.brendawalton.com.

Aida Haron
I am from Singapore. Ten years ago when paper crafting took off in earnest I became a member of the design team at a local store. Sizzix was included in their inventory, and that opened a new dimension to crafting for me. The role of in-store demonstrator and educator gave me the opportunity to explore die-cutting even further. I hope this book will be a source of wonderful ideas. Happy crafting! Visit my blog: Life and Paper Crafting at www.aidaharon.com.

Anna Redfern
I have been crafting in some form or another all of my life. Recently I discovered blogging and papercrafting and now my days are filled with the joy of craft! I love working in 3-D and mixed-media and I work on several design teams. My favorite designers (Eileen Hull, Wendy Vecchi, and Tim Holtz) certainly provide me with plenty of inspiration!

Cara Mariano
I have been creating designs for as long as I can remember and currently spend my days working as the art director for Ellison. I enjoy spending time with my husband, Glenn, and our two kids, Aubrey and Drew. When I am not planning the next fun event for my kids, my free time is spent taking pictures. I have a passion for making fun, inexpensive projects that my friends and family can enjoy.

Anna-Karin Evaldsson
I started papercrafting in 2002. How lucky I am to have found the joy of making art from paper, dies, stamps, ink, and paint. I enjoy switching between different types of projects and trying out new techniques. Every project is a creative adventure and the possibilities are truly endless. Find me at my blog: www.layersofink.blogspot.com.

Anna Wight
I have a love for nature and everything artsy, including photography. Our critters are often featured on my blog SweetMissDaisy.Typepad.com. A few of my favorite things include chickens, snowmen, sunflowers, coffee, the Pacific Coast, and autumn. I am also proud to be a stamp illustrator for Whipper Snapper Designs. Cluck, cluck!

Deena Ziegler
I am a mom, wife, daughter, sister, and friend. And when I am not busy making memories about all of those things I am crafting and blogging about all of those things. I started as a professional crafter 14 years ago. Any day you can find me in my craft room designing, traveling for Sizzix, teaching at my local store or online; or drawing, painting, creating, and running my card kit business. Connect with me on my blog www.deenaziegler.typepad.com.

Diana Hetherington

I am a mixed-media artist in Fredericton, New Brunswick, Canada. I have a background in the school of getting grungy, inky, and all around dirty. I am a local instructor/teacher and am currently a design team member for Eileen Hull's Inspiration team and Artist on the Block. Nothing brings me more joy than sharing with others on my Instagram feed, Facebook page, and website: all of which you can find by keying missusgmoments.com in your web browser.

Hilary Kanwischer

I live in South Florida, with my two children, where I work as a firefighter by day, and mad crafter by night. I have a serious love for holidays and I've been known to create Christmas ornaments in May and Halloween decor in June. I have been so blessed to have had the opportunity to design for some amazing companies over the last 10 years, my favorite being Sizzix, because it has opened a whole new world of crafting for me through die-cutting. My dream is to move to Vermont and open a country store one day. Stop by my blog at: www.hilaryscraps.typepad.com.

Jeanne Streiff

I have been a crafter since I was old enough to hold a crayon. I have worked as a designer for great companies since 2005 and my projects have been published in several books, magazines, and product catalogs. I have been married over 30 years to my husband, Joe, and we have four sons. We live in the great state of Texas with our dogs, ducks, and chickens. You can see my latest creations at www.inkypaws.blogs. splitcoaststampers.com.

Eileen Hull

I grew up in a large family where an art project was always in the works. Learning to think creatively has benefited me throughout my life: from 13 military moves and raising four children to developing product lines for craft manufacturers. In 2009, Sizzix launched my signature line of ScoreBoards™ dies. My 10th Sizzix collection was released in February, 2014. I also have a line of innovative inks called ColorBox™ Blends with Clearsnap. Visit my blog: eileenhull.com.

Jan Hobbins

I am from Edmonton, Alberta, Canada. My husband Rob and I have three grown children, all designers! I have been an avid crafter, sewer, and artist my whole life, but discovered scrapbooking in 2005. My sister and her friend purchased a scrapbook store, asked me to come work for them, and I was instantly addicted. Sizzix asked me to join their Design Team in 2012 and I have loved every minute of it.

Jennifer Priest

My crafting journey started with beading and jewelry when I was 9 years old. These days I share my love of creativity, DIY, and practical living here at Just JP, on the Hydrangea Hippo YouTube Channel, via social media, and through my online classes. On the business side, I run the consulting firm Rainmaker Media Works, providing social media management services and blogger outreach for craft product manufacturers as well as coaching services to artists and makers.

Janette Daneshmand

I am a craft designer, snail mail artist, and the creator of Pocket Letters™, an organized and artful way to send penpal letters around the world. I have a penchant for planners, paper crafts, making YouTube videos, thrifting, and hamburgers! I am inspired by my faith and the world around me, and always look for the humor and beauty in everyday life. I believe it's the "little things" that make life BIG! Please visit www.janettelane.blogspot.com or www.pocketletterpals.com.

Jessica Roe

I am the founder and editor-in-chief of *Everyday Party Magazine*. As far back as high school I loved to throw elaborate parties, even hosting and designing my junior/senior prom! After my sons were born, I went back to my party love and now design immersive themed parties. Check out my designs on my website: everydaypartymag.com to help inspire the bash of your dreams!

Kylie Jenkins

I am a former marine biology major and paralegal turned owner, creative director, blogger, party stylist, graphic designer, baker, seamstress, glitter fairy, and magic maker for my two children. Many of my styled projects and parties are in Mingle Magazine and Tattle Magazine, and online including Martha Stewart's Dreamers into Doers, Celebrate Magazine, & Hostess with the Mostess. I work with Create UR Plate, Tiny Prints, Jelly Belly Company, World Market, and Koyal Wholesale, and I am on the Sizzix Design Team!

Laura Russell

I am the creator and owner of Make Life Lovely, a creative blog where I share craft tutorials, fabulous parties, DIY projects, home décor ideas, and more. My projects have been published in multiple magazines and featured on many popular websites such as Martha Stewart, Good Housekeeping, BuzzFeed, Disney Baby, Babble, and more. I love creating as a member of the Sizzix Design Team. I live with my husband and four children in San Diego. Visit www.makelifelovely.com.

Jo Packham

In the publishing industry for more than 30 years, I have authored, compiled, or packaged more than 1,000 titles. In partnership with Stampington & Co., we publish the bestselling magazines *Where Women CREATE*, *Where Women COOK*, and *Where Women Create BUSINESS*. My imprint WWC PRESS, publishes titles with Quarry Books authored by the leading how-to, food, and business experts in the world. I partner with Sizzix on a line of dies for the foodies and party planners/givers. Visit: www.wherewomencreate.com.

Laura French

I have long enjoyed crafting, sewing, painting and calligraphy. For many years I worked part–time for Printworks Collection, designing and teaching classes on weekends, all while I kept my day job in the corporate world. My favorite quote: "Nothing is all good or all bad," by Dennis Praeger.

Lisa Hoel

I am blessed to be married to the greatest guy in the world and have two dynamic boys. I am a graphic designer and I have never met a craft I didn't like, and papercrafting is no exception. I am inspired by my family, life and God's creation all around us. I hope I can have a small part in inspiring you!

Katie Farmer

I am a graphic designer, party stylist, and the owner of Celebration Lane, an online party shop selling invitations, party supplies, balloons, and gifts. I love entertaining friends, crafting, designing new printables, and spending time with my family at Disney. Visit me: www.celebrationlane.com.

Lori Whitlock

After several years of working in a design studio, I found my true passion developing products for the crafting industry. Over the past 10 years, I have designed for many prominent companies in our industry. I currently license paper designs and fabric, as well as digital cutting files and scrapbooking files. Sizzix proudly welcomes me as a licensed designer for its brand new assortment of designs to enhance cardmaking, scrapbooking, home décor and other handmade crafts. You can learn more about me at www.loriwhitlock.com

Michele Muska

I work in the craft, needle arts, and quilting industry. I serve on the executive board of two nonprofit organizations, The Quilt Alliance and International Quilt Association. I am an author and a fiber artist who also loves to work in mixed-media and paper arts. My work is featured in many national magazines, books and on public TV. You can learn more at www.lolarae.com.

Rina Gonzales

I am the owner of Mothership Scrapbook Gal, a craft business based in Riverside, California, with a mission to help people craft their special and everyday moments through craft events, DIY card kits, and custom orders. I am best known for my "Crafty Happy Hour" event where crafters of all levels and ages come together and create greeting cards. No experience is required, and all supplies are provided. Visit me: mothershipscrapbookgal.com.

Michelle Stewart

I am a party loving mom of three boys, party stylist, party stationery designer, and craft enthusiast. I share my ideas and passion for parties, DIY, and papercrafting in my blog at Michellespartyplanit.com.

Pam Bray

Hi ... my name is Pam but my closest friends call me Pammejo. I reside in the Memphis Tennessee area ... home of Blues and BBQ. I am a wife to an amazing man who supports my creative endeavors, mom of four, and grandma to nine grandchildren. I love papercrafting, altered projects, and making cards. I am currently on several wonderful design teams which includes Eileen Hull's Inspiration Team using her fabulous Sizzix dies.

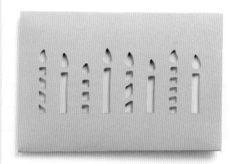

Nicole Wright

I'm a Canadian crafter living in Calgary, AB. I have been crafting for about 20 years and along the way my style is always evolving. I love learning new techniques and sharing. I have met so many people over the years through my blog and had many great opportunities. Including winning Sizzix Who Are You Contest becoming North America's Top Crafter for 2014. Get Inky!

Pamela Alexander

I love creating and designing custom décor and events for my company JP Alexander Events where we specialize in events for the young and the young-at-heart. I reside in North Texas with my husband, six children, and two dogs. Learn more about me at jpalexanderevents.blogspot.com.

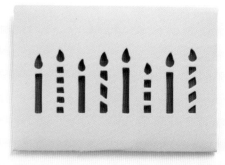

Wanda Guess
I started my paper crafting journey 21 years ago when I discovered the joy of rubber stamping. My first creative love was photography. I currently enjoy all types of papercrafting, but cardmaking is my passion. I have been blogging for six years and recently started my own company called Stampcat Studio. I live in beautiful Northern California with my husband and our orange tabby. Visit me: www.ablogcalledwanda.com

Sandi Genovese
I design dies for Ellison/ Sizzix and author books on cardmaking and scrapbooking. I have been a guest on television shows including *Good Morning America* and *The View*. I hosted my own show on the DIY and HGTV networks from 2001 through 2010. I write a hobbies syndicated newspaper column and license my designs for sale in stores and on QVC and HSN. I consult with craft and education companies about hosting how-to videos on their websites as well as on my own at sandigenovese.com.

Stephanie Ackerman
I am an ordinary girl living an extraordinary life where I get to do what I love for a living. My purpose is to create, inspire, teach, and encourage others through creative arts. I love to make because God created and gave me specific gifts and talents. HE is the reason for my ART so that is why you will always see (or maybe not see) a HEart in my work. I invite you to my blog at: www.homegrownhospitality.typepad.com.

Wendy Cuskey
I have been scrapbookin for over 10 years. I enjoy creating mini albums as unique gifts, to showcase summer beach days, and to remember the family vacations I've enjoyed with my husband, two boys, and my Yorkie. After working in the legal field fo over 20 years, I transitioned into my job a Sizzix and know I am truly blessed to hav found employment where I can practice m passion each and every day.

Sharyn Sowell
I am a mixed-media artist and author. I authored: "Paper cutting Techniques for Scrapbooks and Cards and Silhouettes", design stickers for Ms. Grossman, fabric for Clothworks Textiles, and rubber stamps for Clearsnap. I also design for Hallmark, Sunrise Greetings, Creative Converting, York Wall coverings, and Michaels. I have twice been awarded the Louie Award, the Oscar of the greeting card industry. Visit: sharynsowell.com and sharynsowellartblog.blogspot.com.

Tiffany Johnson
I am the crafter behind iheartartblog.com. An army wife and mom of 3, I am currently stationed in New Orleans, Louisiana. I love all things paper and ink and can be found traveling, running, trying new local restaurants, and reading between crafting sessions.

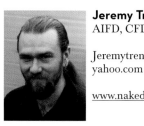

Jeremy Trentelman
AIFD, CFD, UPFA

Jeremytrentelman.aifd@ yahoo.com

www.nakedpetals.com

Design Manager - Olive & Dahlia
Immediate Past President, UPFA
CDF Committee, AIFD
PR Committee, SW Region AIFD

Index